BERTABEAN:

A Storybook about Self-Esteem for Grown-Up Girls

Kate Carpenter

Copyright 2006

PROLOGUE

Once upon a time...
As bizarre as it may seem...
Lived a very gifted woman
With a lack of self-esteem.

For despite Roberta's talent,
And her beauty, and her brains,
She was suffering from an angst
That only low self-worth explains.

But her introspective nature
Finally led her to a place
Where she vowed to find her demons
And confront them, face-to-face.

So what follows is the story
Of her quest for self-esteem -
And the impact it created
On the life of Bertabean.

ONE: WISTFULNESS

Berta woke up Monday morning
In the middle of December
More exhausted and unhappy
Than she ever could remember.

Every bone in Berta's body
Had acquired a constant ache -
She was coiled up with a tension
That she couldn't seem to shake.

Underneath it there was sadness -
Was it longing …or regret?
Maybe menopause was causing
Her anxiety - and yet …

Berta's doctor had assured her
This was not the dreaded "change" –
Could it be a mid-life crisis
Making Berta feel so strange?

Was this just some silly phase
She would eventually outgrow?
Or was something really wrong here?
Berta simply didn't know.

Then she heard a school bus stopping
At the corner up the street -
And it brought back happy memories
Of a time when life was sweet.

Plaid wool skirts and penny loafers...
Noisy halls and tardy bells...
Morning intercom announcements...
Hot lunch cafeteria smells…

Purple mimeographed instructions
With the ink still slightly wet...
Auditorium assemblies...
Someone's squeaky clarinet…

Silver metal pencil sharpeners
Mounted next to classroom doors…
And the pungent smell of paste wax
On the old linoleum floors.

Looking back on all these memories,
Bertabean began to cry -
She remembered being happy,
But she couldn't remember why.

Still - in light of all the turmoil
She was currently going through -
Berta thought perhaps the answer
Would provide her with a clue.

So she pulled herself together
In an effort to find out
What this bittersweet nostalgia
For the past was all about.

Then she heard the yellow school bus
Grind its gears and pull away -
And she wished she could be on it -
Just for one more happy day.

TWO: UNCERTAINTY

As a student, my friend Berta
Was among the very best -
She could master any subject
And excel on any test.

In the classroom, she was eager
And articulate and bright -
And when called on for an answer,
She was almost always right.

Now - although she couldn't remember
Facts and figures she had learned -
She recalled the recognition
That her good performance earned.

Her achievements were commended
And respected and admired -
And they gained her the approval
That her self-esteem required.

So that sultry day in summer
When the final school bell rang -
And she closed her empty locker
With one last metallic clang -

Berta faced her unknown future
With anxiety and dread;
What was hailed as her "commencement"
Felt like sudden death instead.

There was no one there to give her
An assignment to complete -
No instructions she could follow -
No requirements to meet…

No more mandates and directives
All spelled out in black and white -
No more standardized criteria
To determine wrong from right…

No more subjects to be mastered
With her usual finesse -
No more classmates to compete with -
No more teachers to impress.

In this baffling situation,
What was Bertabean to do?
Without someone there to tell her,
Berta didn't have a clue.

Up to this point, her achievements
Had been based on being "good" -
Doing, thinking, and responding
As obedient children should.

Meeting others' expectations
Was the only role she knew -
And she happened to be good at
What they wanted her to do.

So Roberta went to college
Without any concrete goal
But the comfort and the safety
Of an academic role.

THREE: DISILLUSIONMENT

It was similar to high school,
But it wasn't quite the same -
Out of fifteen hundred students,
Just a handful knew her name.

No one cared about her progress -
Or her 4-point GPA -
And the praise that she was seeking
Never seemed to come her way.

Now, with four more years behind her -
And a Liberal Arts degree -
Berta still had no idea of
What she really wanted to be.

With no driving motivation
To pursue a real career,
Getting married seemed the only good
Alternative from here.

So she made the big transition
Into married life with ease -
Finding pseudo-self-fulfillment
With a man that she could please.

When he woke up every morning,
Berta had his coffee brewed;
When he came home every evening,
Berta served his favorite food.

In between, she scrubbed and polished,
Swept and dusted, waxed and mopped;
She did dishes, she did laundry,
She did gardening, and she shopped.

Bertabean was working harder
Than she'd ever worked before -
But at some point, Berta's husband
Didn't notice anymore.

Pretty soon he took for granted
This one-woman maintenance crew -
And the only things he noticed
Were the things she *didn't* do.

There was no appreciation
For the efforts that she made -
She felt cheated and neglected
And exploited … and afraid.

She had entered into marriage
Seeking comfort and contentment -
And had ended up with nothing
But frustration and resentment.

And along with these emotions,
Berta felt a twinge of shame -
She was wasting her potential,
And had only herself to blame.

After several years of marriage,
She was forced to face the fact
That the role of "little woman"
Was a very tiresome act.

FOUR: DISMAY

With an optimistic outlook,
Berta sought professional work -
And she found a paid position
As a paralegal clerk.

She approached her new employment
With a positive attitude -
Feeling sure she'd be rewarded
With respect and gratitude.

But her boss thought weekly paychecks
Were the only thanks required -
And instead of approbation,
All Roberta got was … tired.

Though she still made every effort
To excel at what she did,
There was none of the applause that
This had won her as a kid.

There was none of the approval
Or respect or admiration
That she needed to support a sense
Of personal validation.

So her husband was successful
Selling time-shares in resorts -
And her boss got rich and famous
In the state's judicial courts…

But without her own ambitions,
Future plans, or personal goals,
She was settling for back-seat,
Second-rate, supporting roles.

Her frustration turned to anger,
And her bitterness to ire -
Pleasing people, after all, had been
Roberta's one desire!

Marilyn French's famous saying
"Scratch a woman, find a rage"
Always made her think of trapped and
Angry animals in a cage …

But Roberta's own captivity
Was the self-inflicted kind -
And the key was in the pocket
Of the child she'd left behind.

That emotional attachment
To her academic years -
Still so powerful and poignant
It could bring our girl to tears -

Was indeed the clue she needed
To resolve the paradox
That had put this gifted woman
In her self-imprisoning box.

The conclusion that she came to
Turned nostalgia to regret:
She had never outgrown her childish need
To be the teacher's pet.

FIVE: PRETENSE

Her attempts to be a "pleaser"
Were the ultimate female curse -
She improved the lives of others
While her own life just got worse.

On the surface, Berta's life was
Looking very good indeed -
She had every modern comfort
That a gal could ever need.

Berta's boss and Berta's husband
Might not value her performance -
But she'd found another way to boost
Her waning self-importance.

To society at large, Roberta
Looked like a success -
She had studied how to decorate
And entertain and dress.

From her cul-de-sac McMansion
With attached 3-car garage
To her weekly spa appointment
For a facial and massage …

From her chic designer wardrobe
To her Lexus SUV -
She was in the "1%,"
As all the world could plainly see!

She had hired help to keep her
House immaculately clean -
And its rooms looked like a layout
In a glossy magazine.

She could throw a party worthy
Of a nod from Martha Stewart -
(If your goal was pleasing people,
There was really nothing to it.)

She was driven by the standards
Of the famed "American Dream"-
But it wasn't as fulfilling
As the hype had made it seem.

She'd accepted all those standards
Of material gain as though
They were lessons in a textbook
She was told she had to know.

Berta still was being graded
On what she was being taught -
But now points were based on money
And the goodies that it bought.

Gone from student to consumer,
She kept trying to make the grade -
For the ultimate reward of
Someone else's accolade.

But her need for validation
Wasn't really being met
By her self-indulgent efforts
To remain the teacher's pet.

SIX: SUBMISSION

With external validation
As her motivating force,
It was hardly any wonder
She had strayed so far off course.

She was living life according
To what others deemed "correct"-
Being just above the average …
Being just what you'd expect.

So instead of being passionate,
Creative, and unique,
She was docile and compliant
And obedient and meek.

Her submission to authority
Served her very well in school -
But it didn't make for happy
Grown-up women as a rule.

Berta's life was not a project
To be analyzed and graded -
It was not a class assignment
To be judged or ranked or rated.

These weren't qualified instructors
Calculating Berta's score -
They were people just like Berta -
With opinions … nothing more.

She was using their approval
As her fragile ego's crutch -
But in truth she wasn't certain
That she liked them very much.

Berta's husband was self-centered
And insensitive and aloof -
His "discussions" were a monologue
Of censure and reproof.

Berta's boss was loud and pompous
To the point of being rude -
His demeanor was demeaning
And his people skills were crude.

And as Berta and her husband
Climbed the ladder of success,
Berta found she liked the people
In their circles less and less.

They made Berta feel uneasy -
Though she thought that might be due
To the self-esteem dilemma
She was trying to muddle through.

So she let these peers and colleagues
Set the standards for success
By assuming they had knowledge
She herself did not possess.

The majority of "Boomers" -
Over 70 million strong -
Had equated wealth with happiness…
But what if they were wrong?

SEVEN: INTROSPECTION

For Roberta, this façade gave
Only superficial pride -
So she pushed her need for constant
Affirmation to the side.

Once she'd quieted her ego -
And its need to be assured -
Berta noticed that another voice
Was struggling to be heard.

This was something that Roberta
Had been willing to repress
When it didn't suit the people
She was trying to impress.

It was not the part of Berta
That had been reshaped and molded
To win favor and acceptance
As her story had unfolded.

This one didn't think "performing"
Was the object of the game -
It was not in search of anyone's
Approval or acclaim.

Berta's inner voice had always
Been summarily rejected
Every time it told Roberta
Not to do what was expected.

If that little voice had piped up
When Roberta was in school,
She'd have questioned every order
And contested every rule.

So it served her, as a student,
To be docile and compliant -
But it kept the grown Roberta
From becoming self-reliant.

She kept waiting for instructors
To applaud her every move -
But if these folks had the answers,
It was difficult to prove.

The divorce rates kept on climbing,
And addiction stats did, too -
While the stress of life was managed
By a Prozac pill or two.

Polls reported less contentment
Than in decades gone before -
Even though, in terms of assets,
People owned a whole lot more.

So - that little voice was saying -
Maybe genuine self-esteem
Didn't come with the possessions
Of the old American Dream.

It was telling my friend Berta
That the self-esteem she sought
Wasn't factory-manufactured
To be packaged up and bought.

EIGHT: PERSPECTIVE

By week's end she was exhausted -
And though this was nothing new -
With the holidays approaching,
She had twice as much to do.

But in spite of endless chores that
Berta needed to be doing,
She sat down on Friday evening
For some mindless TV viewing.

Out of ninety-seven channels,
Nothing interested her much -
They showed mostly infomercials
And reality shows and such.

So she settled on a movie -
Though she'd seen it once before -
With a happy ending seldom
Seen in real life anymore.

But within the first ten minutes,
She was overwhelmed with ads
Selling everything from cruises
To designer maxi-pads.

There were ads for beer and pretzels -
There were ads for cars and trucks -
And a 3-blade cordless grater
That was only 25 bucks …

Then an ad in search of sponsors
For an orphaned children's fund…
Something shifted in Roberta,
And she sat there slightly stunned.

For the same amount of money,
A *machine* would grate your cheese -
Or a hungry child could eat and
Be protected from disease!

Berta happened to be sitting
By a ten-foot Christmas tree
Halfway buried by the boxes
From her latest shopping spree.

But if suddenly those presents
Were to simply disappear,
They would all survive quite nicely
For at least another year.

They would still be safe and sheltered
And have more than enough to eat -
They'd have medicine and vitamins
And clothes and shoes and heat.

Berta wondered what that pretty
Pile of presents really cost
When you measured it in terms of
Other opportunities lost.

So Roberta took the training
She'd acquired in legal research -
Booting up her home computer
To begin her internet search.

NINE: DISGRACE

In the span of just an hour,
Berta saw to what extent
All the money blown on Christmas
Had been tragically misspent.

For her husband's cashmere sweater,
Berta could have bought the seeds
To provide a hundred families
With a year's nutritional needs.

For the book she bought her father -
Full of useless golf advice -
There were five malnourished people
Missing half a ton of rice.

Just the paper and the ribbons
And enclosure cards alone
Could have bought a hungry family
Several chickens of their own.

Over thirty thousand people
Died of hunger everyday -
While she dined on veal piccata
With a glass of Chardonnay.

This did not include the people
Who were dying due to AIDS -
Or to cruel domestic violence -
Or to torture in stockades.

And it wasn't only people
Who were dying every day -
The destruction of the planet
Was decidedly underway.

There was something radically wrong
With this frenetic quest for more
When it came with such indifference
To the planet and the poor.

All that stuff on which Roberta's
Shaky self-esteem was built
Now gave Berta an alarming,
Overwhelming sense of guilt.

All those fine designer labels -
And the Lexus SUV -
Left embarrassment and shame
Where Berta's ego used to be.

The approval she'd been seeking -
And the stature - and the rank -
And the "self-esteem" that came from
Having money in the bank -

Seemed to suddenly be having
Quite the opposite effect:
It was undermining what was
Left of Berta's self-respect.

Now it seemed almost immoral -
Such a big, excessive waste!
And instead of self-esteem,
All she was feeling was…

…disgraced.

TEN: REPROACH

Sunday morning she was restless
And got up at quarter to five;
So as not to wake her husband,
She slipped out to take a drive.

Berta headed north on Broad Street
To her favorite quiet spot
In a local cemetery
That she visited quite a lot.

Here the gates were always open,
So she found a place to park -
And she waited for the sunrise
In the early morning dark.

As she sipped her mug of coffee,
Berta listened to the sounds
Of the whispering of the pine trees
On the peaceful, sacred grounds.

Bertabean began to wonder
What her epitaph would be
If her death should come upon her
Very unexpectedly.

Berta hoped, of course, the phrase
Would be both flattering and kind -
But despite her contemplation
Nothing readily came to mind.

She was really very selfish -
Very vain and very proud -
And for all the same wrong reasons
As the whole consumer crowd.

Though she owned the latest gadgets,
And she drove a fancy car,
She had certainly not been living
An authentic life so far.

She was certainly not creative -
Neither passionate nor unique -
Her conformity was boring,
Unimaginative, and bleak.

She had traded her identity
For a lot of pricey "stuff" -
But she'd reached a critical crossroads,
And her verdict was … *enough*.

This conspicuous consumption
Was decidedly not the way -
And it clearly wasn't working
For Roberta anyway.

For despite her childish reasoning,
Real success was not a score -
Life was not about exam grades
Or report cards anymore.

She no longer was a student
But a woman fully grown –
And the only real approval
Berta needed was her own.

ELEVEN: RESOLUTION

As the sun came up that morning
On a day both bright and fair -
Light came glittering through the pine trees,
And the words were finally there.

When her epitaph was chosen,
Berta wanted it to say
That her innermost convictions
Were her compass every day …

And she'd left the so-called "safety"
Of society's comfort zone
To pursue authentic, heart-felt,
Personal standards all her own.

It was time to reexamine
The decisions she had made -
All the roles she had assumed and
All the parts that she had played.

She could not undo the choices
Or mistakes that she had made -
But she also wasn't willing
To continue this charade.

She was in a loveless marriage -
And a boring job to boot -
Just to fund her poor, pathetic,
Failing self-esteem pursuit.

The integrity that Berta
Was at last inclined to seek
Put her marriage and employment
Up for serious critique.

For by staying in the marriage,
She was living with a lie -
And her law firm peddled "justice"
Only wealthy folks could buy.

With the truth that she was facing,
Berta had to make a choice
That required her to listen
To that little inner voice.

She would have to find her way in
Some new, unexplored direction -
Though it surely meant she'd suffer
Disapproval and rejection.

It would take some big decisions,
And the changes would be hard -
There'd be plenty of opinions
That she'd have to disregard.

But the payoff would be worth it
If she wanted to redeem
What was left of her disintegrating
Sense of self-esteem.

She might sacrifice approval,
But she wouldn't sell her soul
To accept a life on overdrive -
Or worse - remote control.

TWELVE: REDEMPTION

I saw Berta six months later
And was in for a surprise -
I could see a new resilience
And contentment in her eyes.

She was living very simply
In a one-room, walk-up flat -
And for company she'd traded in
Her husband for a cat!

She had left the famous law firm -
And was earning half the pay -
But was working very happily
At the local SPCA.

She was sponsoring two small children
In a country far away -
And the local women's shelter
Got a portion of her pay.

She had given up completely
On the old American Dream -
And although to me her lifestyle
Seemed both radical and extreme …

Even I could see the wisdom
Of the changes she'd embraced -
I was troubled, when I left her,
Of the choices that I faced …

I was suddenly embarrassed
By the vanity and greed
That had taken me so far beyond
My own essential need.

I was still a part of the problem -
But Roberta, the solution -
And that fact inspired me
To make a personal resolution.

For my life was never peaceful
Or contented or serene -
It was stressful and unhappy
And conspicuously obscene.

It was all about the money
And the things that it could buy -
And because of my friend Berta,
I began to wonder ... *Why?*

Was I putting on a show for
Other people's admiration?
Was I using their approval
For my personal validation?

I was certainly not as happy
As Roberta seemed to be -
And the path that I was following
Now seemed very wrong to me.

I decided I would take some steps
To help me simplify -
I could not predict the outcome,
But I knew I had to try.

EPILOGUE

In the end, I came to value
Her advice on self-esteem -
It was truly as empowering
As my friend had made it seem.

Berta said it's just "esteem" that
Other people give to you -
"*Self*-esteem" is inner pride in
Who you are and what you do.

When you start to live the values
That are truest to your heart,
The illusions of approval
Will begin to fall apart.

If you have the faith and courage
To dismiss that childish dream,
You can start the wondrous journey
To authentic self-esteem.

Other books by Kate Carpenter:

Lilabean: A Storybook about
Simplicity for Grown-Up Girls

Ginabean: A Storybook about
Success for Grown-Up Girls

ENUFF: Eliminate the Needless,
Useless, Foolish, and Frivolous

How to Open a Successful Thrift Shop

www.ingramcontent.com/pod-product-compliance
Lightning Source LLC
Chambersburg PA
CBHW062126040426
42337CB00044B/4359